DREAM JOBS IN TECHNOLOGY

COLIN HYNSON

Crabtree Publishing Company
www.crabtreebooks.com

Crabtree Publishing Company
www.crabtreebooks.com
1-800-387-7650

Published in Canada
616 Welland Ave.
St. Catharines, ON
L2M 5V6

Published in the United States
PMB 59051
350 Fifth Ave. 59th Floor
New York, NY

Published in 2017 by CRABTREE PUBLISHING COMPANY

First published in 2016 by Wayland
(A division of Hachette Children's Books)
Copyright © Wayland 2016

Author:
Colin Hynson

Editors:
Victoria Brooker
Jon Richards
Petrice Custance

Designer:
Darren Jordan

Proofreader:
Wendy Scavuzzo

Print and production coordinator:
Katherine Berti

Photo credits

2 Dreamstime.com/Eugensergeev; 3 Dreamstime.com/Eduard Bonnin Turina; 4 Dreamstime.com/Kts; 5t NASA, 5c Dreamstime.com/Maislam; 6b Dreamstime.com/Mimagephotography, 6–7 Dreamstime.com/Wavebreakmedia Ltd; 8–9 Dreamstime.com/Georgil Dolgykh, 9 Dreamstime.com/Mast3r; 10b Anna Frodesiak, 10–11 Dreamstime.com/Jesse Lee Lang, 12 Dreamstime.com/Dacstyle, 12–13 Dreamstime.com/Mast3r; 14b Dreamstime.com/sasalan999, 14–15 Dreamstime.com/Martinmark; 16b Dreamstime.com/Urii Stepanov, 16–17 Dreamstime.com/Dmitriy Shironosov; 18t Dreamstime.com/Igor Akimov, 18–19 Dreamstime.com/Eduard Bonnin Turina; 20 Dreamstime.com/Belahoche, 21c Dreamstime.com/Sigur1, 21t Jeremykemp; 23c Dreamstime.com/Eugensergeev, 23b Dreamstime.com/Vladgalenko; 24–25 Dreamstime.com/Dikliy; 26b NASA, 26–27 NASA, 27t NASA; 28–29 Dreamstime.com/Donvictorio; 31 Dreamstime.com/Georgil Dolgykh.

Library and Archives Canada Cataloguing in Publication

Hynson, Colin, author
Dream jobs in technology / Colin Hynson.

(Cutting-edge careers in STEM)
Issued in print and electronic formats.
ISBN 978-0-7787-2967-9 (hardback).--ISBN 978-0-7787-2990-7 (paperback).--
ISBN 978-1-4271-1863-9 (html)

1. Technology--Vocational guidance--Juvenile literature.
I. Title.

T65.3.H96 2016   j602.3   C2016-906642-8
                                        C2016-906643-6

Library of Congress Cataloging-in-Publication Data

CIP available at the Library of Congress.

Printed in Hong Kong/012017/BK20161024

CONTENTS

TECHNOLOGY

JOBS IN TECHNOLOGY

A CAREER IN TECHNOLOGY WILL EQUIP YOU TO CREATE EVERYTHING FROM SPECIAL EFFECTS IN MOVIES TO SPACE PROBES.

Welcome to the world of working in technology. Studying technology opens doors to a whole range of interesting, exciting, unusual, and amazing jobs! A job in technology doesn't mean you'll be stuck in a laboratory or staring at a computer screen. You could be working in **artificial intelligence**, **nanotechnology,** or video games. This book will help you find out what each job is all about, as well as the rewards of doing the job.

▶ Nanobots may be able to use microtechnology to cure diseases that are currently untreatable by conventional medicine.

SUBJECTS AND QUALIFICATIONS

For each job, you'll see what subjects you may need to study as you move through school, and what further training you will need. These are quite general, as the qualifications for each stage of education are different depending on the country you live in.

▼ Space probes use the latest technology to explore the far reaches of the solar system.

▶ A job in technology can lead to a career at one of the world's leading companies, such as Apple.

Apple Campus
One Infinite Loop

YOU MAY NEED TO STUDY:

THE ROUTE TO

SECONDARY SCHOOL:
Education from about ages 14 to 18

A JOB IN TECHNOLOGY

POST-SECONDARY: Studying for an **undergraduate** degree and a post-graduate degree, such as a **master's degree** and a doctorate

STEM STANDS FOR **S**CIENCE, **T**ECHNOLOGY, **E**NGINEERING, AND **M**ATH. AS SCIENCE, TECHNOLOGY, AND ENGINEERING INDUSTRIES GROW, THERE IS INCREASING DEMAND FOR PEOPLE WITH STEM SKILLS.

BUILDING A CLOUD

CLOUD ARCHITECTS ARE HELPING TO SHAPE THE DIGITAL WORLD.

Cloud computing is one of the fastest-growing parts of the world of **information technology** (IT), and offers a lot of exciting opportunities for anyone who wants a job in computer science. Cloud computing lets you store data or run software over the Internet, rather than on a **hard drive**. This means that you can access information wherever you are.

▼ Using the cloud allows you to store thousands of digital photos and access them from any digital device.

▼ With data stored on the cloud, your computer hard drive can be smaller, making your computer lighter and more portable.

WHAT YOU DO

The working day of a cloud architect will be varied. Even though much of your time will be spent designing and creating the cloud platform, you will also be part of a team looking after the computer needs of the organization you are working for. If you are working for a large organization, there will be plenty of chances to work at different locations, in different places, and with a lot of different people.

THERE ARE THREE TYPES OF CLOUD. THERE IS THE PUBLIC CLOUD, WHICH ANYONE CAN ACCESS, THE PRIVATE CLOUD, WHICH ONLY CERTAIN PEOPLE CAN ACCESS, AND THE HYBRID CLOUD, WHICH IS A COMBINATION OF THE TWO.

WHERE YOU WORK

Just about every large organization and business is either using cloud computing or is moving over to it. This means that you can combine your expertise in computers with any other interest or passion you might have. If you are interested in music, sports, or films, you can work in cloud computing and be part of that industry.

YOU MAY NEED TO STUDY:

THE ROUTE TO

SECONDARY SCHOOL:
Math, science, and computer science

CLOUD COMPUTING

POST-SECONDARY: Computer science. Some universities offer advanced degrees (called master's degrees) in cloud computing.

7

IN 2013, 7 PERCENT OF ALL DATA WAS STORED IN THE CLOUD. BY THE END OF 2016, ABOUT 36 PERCENT WILL BE STORED.

DEVELOPING APPS

THE GROWTH IN MOBILE TECHNOLOGY IS GOOD FOR ANYONE WHO WANTS TO DEVELOP APPS.

8

As an **app** developer, you would create the **code** that runs an app. You might also be involved in designing the look of the app, as well as researching how people will want to use it. Once the app has been created, you may be involved in testing it to make sure that it works properly. Even after the app has been released, you will still have to keep working on it. The world of app development is fast-moving, and you will need to keep your app up to date.

WHAT YOU DO

Your working day will change as your app develops. While you are creating the app, you will be spending a lot of time at your desk writing the code needed for the app. When the app is being tested and is then released to the public, you may find yourself moving between working at your desk and working with others as part of a team.

▲ Apps allow smartphones and tablets to carry out a wide range of tasks, from showing you recipes and cooking techniques to ordering taxis and plotting routes.

EMPLOYERS MAY ASK IF YOU HAVE MADE ANY APPS BEFORE. THIS WILL SHOW THEM THAT YOU HAVE SOME UNDERSTANDING ABOUT HOW APPS WORK AND HOW TO MAKE THEM. YOU CAN PROBABLY START MAKING YOUR OWN SIMPLE APPS AT SECONDARY OR POST-SECONDARY SCHOOL.

THE ROUTE TO
APP DEVELOPMENT

YOU MAY NEED TO STUDY:

SECONDARY SCHOOL: Math, science (especially physics), computer science, and art and design

POST-SECONDARY: Computer science. There are some universities that offer classes in app development as part of a degree in computer science.

95%

▶ As an app developer, you're likely to be part of a team. But there are many apps that are created by a single person.

THERE ARE ROUGHLY ABOUT THREE MILLION APPS AVAILABLE— BUT THAT NUMBER IS GROWING BY 2,000 EVERY DAY.

WHERE YOU WORK

Many of the businesses and organizations that use apps do not produce the apps themselves. They usually work with a company that specializes in creating apps. If you work for one of these companies, you'll find that the kind of work you're involved in is really varied. You might be working at your local zoo one day, then the next day you'll be at a major film studio working on an app for their next blockbuster movie.

INFERNO ARTIST

A VISUAL EFFECTS ARTIST CREATES MOVIE SCENES THAT WOULD BE TOO DANGEROUS, TOO EXPENSIVE, OR JUST IMPOSSIBLE TO FILM.

As a Visual Effects Artist (also known as an Inferno Artist) you will create movie special effects using computer-generated imagery (CGI). Visual Effects Artists need to have both technological and artistic skills. Every movie is planned using a **storyboard**. Once this has been finalized, you will be able to see where the **visual effects** are needed. Visual Effects Artists are not normally involved with the actual filming. Your work really begins when filming ends, a stage that's called **post–production**.

▲ A storyboard is a series of drawings that show the story behind the film being made.

WHAT YOU DO

There are a lot of different people who are involved with the post–production part of a movie or television program. This means that your typical working day will be a mixture of being in front of a computer creating the visual effects you have been asked to create, as well as working with everybody else involved in post–production. Visual Effects Artists are sometimes asked to work long hours to fit in with the schedule for the movie or television program.

IF YOU ARE WORKING WITH A BIG POST-PRODUCTION COMPANY, YOU MAY HAVE THE CHANCE TO SPECIALIZE IN A PARTICULAR AREA OF SPECIAL EFFECTS, SUCH AS CREATING FANTASTIC LANDSCAPES.

WHERE YOU WORK

Although you might expect to work for a film or television company, most visual effects artists work for companies that specialize in providing post–production expertise. If you work for one of these companies, you'll be involved in all sorts of different projects where visual effects are needed. One day you might be creating special effects for a major movie, and the next day the visual effects for a new car commercial.

▼ This mountain scene was created using CGI and may be placed behind actors in post-production. This way they can film in a studio rather than on location, which may be more expensive.

YOU MAY NEED TO STUDY:

THE ROUTE TO

SECONDARY SCHOOL: Science (especially physics), math, computer science, and art and design

VISUAL EFFECTS ARTIST

POST-SECONDARY: There are some universities that offer degrees in computer animation and visual effects. However, a degree in computer science is also useful.

DIGITAL PROTECTION

FIGHT CRIME WITH SOME SERIOUS TECH SKILLS AND QUALIFICATIONS.

12 **Cybercrime** takes a lot of different forms, and affects everyone from large businesses to individual people. If you want to be in the front line of the defense against cybercrime, you can work in **cybersecurity**. Your main job will be to try to protect computer information by using tools such as **firewalls** (which block **malware** from getting into a computer), or creating **encryption** codes.

```
Aircrack PTW cont
                    Aircrack-
  [00:02:05] Tested 11238 keys
epth   byte(vote)
/ 16   77(24320)  D9(24320)  7E(24064)
/ 7    91(24064)  4E(23808)  AB(23808)
/ 3    39(27392)  8B(26368)  BD(26368)
/ 7    38(26112)  8C(25600)  87(24832)
/ 5    30(26880)  4D(26880)  FC(25856)
        KEY FOUND! [ 77:34:39:38:
ecrypted correctly: 100%
```

◄ Part of your time will be spent trying to crack your own encryption to try to find any weaknesses.

WHAT YOU DO

The methods used by cybercriminals are constantly changing, so part of your job will involve keeping up with changing methods of cybercrime. There are new malware threats appearing all the time and they are getting better at breaking through firewalls and hiding themselves on a computer network so that people don't know they are there. You'll have to improve the security levels on your computer network to fight off these new threats.

GOVERNMENTS ARE OFFERING IMAGINATIVE WAYS TO GET YOUNG PEOPLE INTERESTED IN DIGITAL PROTECTION. FOR EXAMPLE, THE DEPARTMENT FOR HOMELAND SECURITY IN THE UNITED STATES HOLDS CYBERSECURITY CAMPS AND STUDY DAYS.

THE ROUTE

YOU MAY NEED TO STUDY:

SECONDARY SCHOOL:
Science, math, and computer science

TO CYBERSECURITY

POST-SECONDARY:
Computer science or math

WHERE YOU WORK

As cybersecurity becomes more important, the number of businesses that specialize in protecting computer networks is growing. They can protect the computer networks of large and small organizations. People in cybersecurity can also work for the armed forces, the police, or for security services.

▶ Much of your time will be spent analyzing attempted attacks by cybercriminals.

IN ONE SINGLE SECURITY BREACH IN 2011, THE PERSONAL DETAILS OF MORE THAN 77 MILLION PEOPLE WERE STOLEN BY HACKERS FROM SONY'S VIDEO GAME ONLINE NETWORK.

THE INTERNET OF THINGS

HELP TO CREATE A WORLD WHERE OBJECTS AND MACHINES TALK TO EACH OTHER.

Imagine a world where there are **smart objects** with computer chips that collect and share information across the Internet. This is called "the Internet of things." As the Internet of things grows, there will be more and more demand for people who can work in a wide range of areas. The collection of enormous amounts of data will lead to career opportunities in cloud computing, cybersecurity, and data analysis.

◄ Bridges can be equipped with sensors that detect traffic levels, and look for signs of wear and tear.

THE ROUTE TO

YOU MAY NEED TO STUDY:

SECONDARY SCHOOL:
Science, math, and computer science

THE INTERNET OF THINGS

POST-SECONDARY: Computer science. Some universities offer classes on the Internet of things as part of a degree in computing.

THERE ARE TECHNOLOGY COMPANIES THAT ARE DEVELOPING WAYS OF USING THE INTERNET OF THINGS TO HELP US LOOK AFTER OUR PETS. "SMART" BOWLS WILL TELL US WHEN OUR CAT OR DOG NEEDS SOME FRESH FOOD.

WHERE YOU WORK

Because the Internet of things can be applied to almost any industry, there are few limitations as to who you could end up working with. It could be a large construction company, or a firm making the latest wearable technology. Every day, new potential career opportunities are opening up in this exciting world.

15

◀ **Smartwatches** can record your exercise routines, monitor your physical health, and send information to your doctor.

WHAT YOU DO

Working in the Internet of things means a lot of variety in your working day. There are many people working in this industry, and you may have to cooperate with all of them. You will be working with the designers and manufacturers of "smart" objects, as well as with people who work on the computing side.

DESIGN THE EXPERIENCE

FIND OUT HOW TECHNOLOGY CAN IMPROVE THE WAY PEOPLE USE THINGS.

16

Every product that we use has been designed. In the digital world, the user experience (UX) designer makes sure that a website, app, or computer game has the right "feel" to it. The UX designer is concerned with the "**findability**" and the "**usability**" of the app. Findability is how easy it is for somebody to find what they are looking for in the app. Usability is about how people will navigate around the app and whether they need any complicated instructions before they start.

YOU WILL CREATE SOMETHING CALLED A **PERSONA** OR A USER MODEL. THIS IS A FICTIONAL CHARACTER THAT WILL HELP WITH THE DESIGN OF THE NEW PRODUCT.

▶ Any app you design must be easy to find and easy to use.

WHAT YOU DO

Your working day as a UX Designer will be varied. Some of your time will be spent in front of a computer creating avatars and **wireframes** for a new product. However, you will also have to be away from your desk quite a lot. UX designers have to organize groups of people to test any prototypes in a lot of different locations.

WHERE YOU WORK

Just about every technology company making digital products such as websites, apps, or games will need the expertise of a UX designer. Larger companies will employ their own UX designers. There are also special companies that supply UX design services to smaller businesses. Many businesses also make sure that the UX designer is the same person who actually designs the product.

▶ Part of your role will be testing products with members of the public to see how they use and react to it.

YOU MAY NEED TO STUDY:

THE ROUTE TO

SECONDARY SCHOOL: Science, math, computer science, and art and design

UX DESIGN

POST-SECONDARY: Computer science, computer–aided design (CAD). There are some universities that offer advanced classes in UX design.

THE ACTUAL DESIGN OF A DIGITAL PRODUCT IS DONE BY A USER INTERFACE (UI) DESIGNER. IF YOU DO BOTH OF THESE JOBS, YOU COULD BE CALLED A VISUAL DESIGNER.

TINY TECH

DESIGN AND BUILD OBJECTS AND MACHINES THAT ARE FAR TOO SMALL TO SEE.

▼ This nanotechnology laboratory in Russia uses highly specialized equipment to create devices and materials.

Engineers and scientists who work in the field of nanotechnology are creating devices and materials on a very small scale. You'll be working with materials between 1 and 100 **nanometers** in size. To give you an idea of how small that is, the thickness of a sheet of paper in this book is about 100,000 nanometers. Nanotechnlogy is being used in a wide range of industries, including computing, energy production, and medicine. Nanotechnologists can produce lighter and stronger materials, and electronic devices that are smaller, faster, and more portable.

WHERE YOU WORK
Because nanotechnology is spreading into so many technology sectors, you'll find that there are plenty of opportunities to work in this area. You may find yourself working for businesses that specialize in electronics, energy production and storage, transportation, materials science, medicine, or food production.

WHAT YOU DO

If you are working as a nanotechnologist, a lot of your time will be spent creating and testing new devices and materials. These materials are usually made in "clean rooms." This means that the area you are working in will be as free as possible from any kind of contaminant, especially dust. Any new devices and materials will still have to be tested outside of the laboratory to make sure they work in the real world. You may be involved in this testing, as well.

YOU MAY NEED TO STUDY:

THE ROUTE TO

SECONDARY SCHOOL: Science (especially physics), math, and computer science

NANOTECHNOLOGY

POST-SECONDARY: Computer science, physics, math, chemistry, materials science. Some universities offer advanced courses in nanotechnology.

19

▲ This flexible transparent screen was created using nanotechnology materials. It could be used to display video calls or movies before being rolled up and put away.

NANOBOTS **ARE TINY DEVICES THAT CAN BE INJECTED INTO A PATIENT AND USED TO HELP REPAIR DAMAGED CELLS, OR TO SEEK OUT AND DESTROY VIRUSES OR CANCER CELLS.**

THINKING MACHINES

TECHNOLOGY SKILLS CAN HELP TO BUILD MACHINES THAT WILL THINK AND ACT FOR THEMSELVES.

▼ Artificial intelligence may also be used to create "smart" artificial limbs.

The rise of artificial intelligence (AI), or machine learning, makes it possible for machines to make decisions themselves. They do not need people to give them instructions. We can already see examples of AI today. Driverless cars are being tested on our roads, and Internet search engines use it to help search the web. AI can also be found in video games and even in some hospitals.

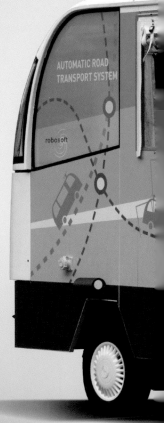

AUTOMATIC ROAD
TRANSPORT SYSTEM

robosoft

THE ROUTE TO ARTIFICIAL INTELLIGENCE

YOU MAY NEED TO STUDY:

SECONDARY SCHOOL: Science, math, and computer science

POST-SECONDARY: Computer science. Some universities offer courses on artificial intelligence as part of their computer science degree.

RESEARCH IS BEING DONE INTO CREATING A "VIRTUAL COMPANION" FOR ELDERLY PEOPLE. IT WILL MONITOR THE HEALTH OF THE PERSON IT IS LOOKING AFTER AND CAN CONTACT MEDICAL SERVICES IF NEEDED.

WHERE YOU WORK

Nearly every technology company is currently looking into how they can use artificial intelligence in their products. If you want to work in AI, you can combine it with another interest, such as medicine, games design, or robotics.

▶ This robot at a hospital in the United States is delivering medicine to where it is needed.

▼ This driverless minibus is being tested on the streets of León, Spain.

CITY DEMONSTRATIONS

CityMobil2

WHAT YOU DO

If you are working in artificial intelligence, you will be spending much of your day developing and testing intelligent machines. This may mean using a computer to write the programming language needed for the machine to operate properly. You will also be involved in the design and creation of the machines themselves, so you will be working with designers and engineers.

DRONE PILOT

THIS TECHNOLOGY CAN TAKE YOU TO THE OTHER SIDE OF THE WORLD, WITHOUT LEAVING YOUR OFFICE.

Drones or Unmanned Aerial Vehicles (UAVs) are planes that fly without a pilot onboard. Drones are used by the military, but are moving into other areas of life, including law enforcement agencies, journalism, and deliveries. Like many technology jobs, working with drones will allow you to combine your love of all things technological with the chance to work in a lot of different areas. The drones of the future have to be designed and built, along with the software used to control them. This software will also have to be continually updated.

▲ This military drone is used to deliver medical supplies to remote bases.

WHAT YOU DO

If you are working with drones, then some of your time will be in the laboratory or factory as part of the team designing and building the aircraft. Different jobs will need different kinds of drones, so you'll be involved in a lot of new projects. Once the drone has been built, you will have to spend some time testing it outside to check that it's working properly.

THE ROUTE TO A CAREER WITH

YOU MAY NEED TO STUDY:

SECONDARY SCHOOL:
Science (especially physics), math, computer science, and design

POST-SECONDARY: Computer science and engineering. There are also drone training colleges that can teach you how to design, build, and control drones.

DRONES

▼ Drones can either be flown by a person on the ground or by using its own computer program.

WHERE YOU WORK
There are a lot of technology companies that are exploring how they may be able to use drones in their work. At the moment, drones are mostly used by the police and armed forces. However, in the future you may find yourself working for delivery companies, TV and film companies, or with organizations helping people in disaster-hit regions.

▶ A **submersible** drone is lowered into a lake.

SOME DRONES DON'T FLY—THEY SWIM! SUBMERSIBLE DRONES HAVE BEEN USED TO SEARCH FOR THE WRECKAGE OF AIRCRAFT THAT HAVE CRASHED FAR OUT AT SEA.

GAMES DEVELOPER

BE PART OF A TECH INDUSTRY THAT'S USED BY MILLIONS OF PEOPLE EVERY DAY.

24

If you are thinking about becoming a games developer, you will have to decide on an area you would like to specialize in. Today's computer games are usually so complex that they require a large team of people working together. You may decide to become a game programmer, creating the code that actually makes the game run. Game designers create the look of the game, developing characters, settings, how the game plays, and the different levels.

WHAT YOU DO

The working day for both game designers and game programmers is office and computer-based. However, because so many people are involved in the creation of a single game, you will be dividing your time between working by yourself and working as part of a team.

THE ROUTE

YOU MAY NEED TO STUDY:

SECONDARY SCHOOL: Science (especially physics), math, computer science, and design

TO GAMES DEVELOPMENT

POST-SECONDARY: Computer games design, computer science, graphic design

WHERE YOU WORK

There are a large number of companies who create computer games. All of them are looking for games developers to meet growing demand for new games. There are plenty of opportunities to work abroad as many of these companies have offices in different countries.

◄ Games developers need to create an experience that is complete with realistic **graphics** and sounds.

THE GLOBAL VIDEO GAMES MARKET IS EXPECTED TO BE WORTH NEARLY $119 BILLION BY 2019.

INTO SPACE

THIS JOB WILL TAKE YOU FAR BEYOND EARTH AND OUT INTO SPACE.

26

On January 19, 2006, a space probe called New Horizons launched from Cape Canaveral, in Florida. Eight years later, it arrived at the dwarf planet Pluto. Onboard were instruments to study the atmosphere and the surface of Pluto, as well as cameras to take pictures. New Horizons is now traveling to the outer reaches of our solar system. Today, most space exploration is carried out by probes, because it is impossible to send people on very long journeys.

▼ The NASA team celebrates when it receives confirmation that New Horizons (right) has reached Pluto.

WHAT YOU DO

If you are involved in a space probe project, your role will change over time. When the space probe is being designed and built, you will be part of a team working both in a laboratory and at **Mission Control** (the place where the flight of the space probe is managed). However, it may take several years for the space probe to reach its destination. During that time, you may work on other projects. Once the probe is near its destination, you will be back in Mission Control to start communicating with the space probe.

SOME SPACE AGENCIES RUN SUMMER CAMPS FOR YOUNG PEOPLE WHERE YOU COULD GET THE CHANCE TO COMMUNICATE WITH A SPACE PROBE AND COME UP WITH IDEAS FOR FUTURE SPACE EXPERIMENTS.

WHERE YOU WORK

If you want to work in the development of space probes, you will probably be working for a government space program. This could be NASA in the United States or the European Space Agency. Canada, Russia, China, Japan, and India also have their own space agencies.

▶ Space probes don't just orbit or fly past planets. Some are rovers that explore the surface of another planet. The Curiosity rover is studying the geology of Mars.

YOU MAY NEED TO STUDY:

THE ROUTE TO

SECONDARY SCHOOL: Science (especially physics), math, and computer science

SPACE PROBE

POST-SECONDARY: Computer science, physics, and planetary science

DEVELOPMENT

ETHICAL HACKING

USE YOUR TECH SKILLS TO BREAK INTO OTHER PEOPLE'S COMPUTERS—LEGALLY!

▼ Many government security organizations, such as the FBI in Washington, D.C. (below), employ hackers to test their own systems.

To protect themselves from **hacking** attacks, some organizations actually organize an attack on their own computer network so they can find any weaknesses. If you are interested in a career in cybersecurity, you might want to become a penetration tester (also called an ethical hacker). You will be asked to organize a hacking attack on a computer network.

WHAT YOU DO

As an ethical hacker, much of your working day will be spent communicating with the people inside the organization whose computer network you are trying to break into. They have to know what you are doing and when you are planning to do it. You will have to spend quite a lot of time planning your hacking activities before you actually start. You will also need to keep up to date with the latest techniques and technologies used by cybercriminals.

IF YOU WANT TO WORK AS AN ETHICAL HACKER, YOU HAVE TO CONVINCE WHOEVER IS HIRING YOU THAT YOU CAN BE TRUSTED. AFTER ALL, YOU ARE TRYING TO BREAK INTO THEIR COMPUTER NETWORK.

IN 2001–2002, GARY MCKINNON FROM THE U.K. HACKED INTO 97 COMPUTERS AT THE U.S. NAVY, ARMY, PENTAGON, AND NASA. HE CLAIMED HE WAS LOOKING FOR GOVERNMENT FILES ABOUT ALIENS.

WHERE YOU WORK

There are a few companies that specialize in offering ethical hacking to businesses. However, you will probably work for a company that offers more general cybersecurity support. Some of the larger technology companies may employ their own cybersecurity staff and this could include people skilled in hacking.

THE ROUTE TO
ETHICAL HACKING

YOU MAY NEED TO STUDY:

SECONDARY SCHOOL: Science (especially physics), math, and computer science

POST-SECONDARY: Computer science

GLOSSARY

APP
Short for "application;" Software that is designed to run on smartphones and tablets

ARTIFICIAL INTELLIGENCE
Computers that can independently perform tasks that usually require human intelligence

CLOUD COMPUTING
Storing and accessing computer data through the Internet rather than from a hard drive

CODE
A set of instructions made up of letters and numbers that is read by computer software

CYBERCRIME
Criminal activities carried out using computers and the Internet

CYBERSECURITY
The technology and practices needed to protect computers from attacks from cybercriminals

DRONE
A vehicle that can be navigated either automatically or from a distance

ENCRYPTION
The conversion of computer data so that it can only be read by selected people

FINDABILITY
The ease with which somebody can find what they want on a piece of software

FIREWALL
A computer security system that controls what is going out of or coming into a computer system

GRAPHICS
The design of images that are used on websites, apps, or advertising

HACKING
Gaining unauthorized access to a computer system

HARD DRIVE
The hard drive controls the use of a hard disk inside a computer.

INFORMATION TECHNOLOGY
The technology involved in the use and maintenance of computer systems, including both the hardware and software

MALWARE
Software designed to disrupt or destroy computer systems

MASTER'S DEGREE
A university degree that is a higher level than a bachelor's degree

MISSION CONTROL
The command center for controlling and supporting space flights

NANOMETER
A very small unit of measurement; A single nanometer is equal to one billionth of a meter.

NANOBOT
A tiny machine with parts that can be measured in nanometers

NANOTECHNOLOGY
The use of technology and engineering at a nanoscale, normally between 1 and 100 nanometers

PERSONA
Personas are created by UX designers; They are fictional characters based on the kind of person who will use a new product.

POST-PRODUCTION
Work done on a film after the filming has been completed

SMART OBJECTS
Everyday objects, such as fridges, that have a computer chip which collects and shares information across the Internet

SMARTWATCHES
A tiny computer worn on the wrist; It can be used for a lot of things, such as monitoring the health of the wearer.

STORYBOARD
A series of drawings created before a film is made. The storyboard shows the story behind a movie.

SUBMERSIBLE
Able to operate underwater

UNDERGRADUATE
A person who is studying at a university for their first degree

USABILITY
This is the measurement of how simple it is to use an app or a piece of software.

VISUAL EFFECTS
The creation of images in a film that cannot be created in a live-action shot

WIREFRAME
A rough layout of a product that is being developed

INDEX